Star
Clothes on eBay

By Michael Larsen

Table of Contents

Preface

Start Selling Clothes on eBay: A beginner's Guide will introduce you to what it takes to get started in the world of selling used clothing online.

For someone looking to earn extra income, this is a great place to start. This book guides you through:

- Why Clothing? A look at what makes pre-owned clothing a good choice to sell online and make money.
- Where to get clothing. Discover the many places to get used clothing, starting with your own closet.
- What it takes to get started. Insight on what equipment is needed to photograph and prepare the clothing.
- How to list items online. Find out what marketplaces are the best for listing clothing for sale and see step-by-step how to list your first pre-owned clothing items online.
- Next steps. Get a look at the next steps for building your clothing sales into a business that will earn you plenty of money.

If you have ever wondered about how to buy and resell clothing online, give it a shot. It is fun and profitable!

Introduction

How I started selling used clothing.

I didn't get into selling clothing intentionally. I needed to earn some extra money but I also needed something flexible as to not interfere with my job. So I started dabbling with on-line selling. I went to garage sales and thrift stores looking for things I could sell on eBay or Amazon. I took pictures and listed things in the evenings and weekends. Looking for things to sell on the weekends. I got to know certain niche markets like used video games, books, clothing and some antiques.

A pattern started to present itself. I was able to consistently sell clothing. The dollar amount of each item I was selling was not sky high but the profit was very good. I might pay $2.50 for a shirt and sell it for $19.00. Not a huge amount but they would add up because of the consistency and volume. So pretty soon after noticing this pattern, I started to focus more on selling clothing. The results were very impressive.

Clothing sold consistently and it was plentiful. I could always find good quality used clothing for reasonable prices. I could go through one rack of shirts at a thrift shop and find several items that were profitable. In a small amount of time I could find a lot of inventory. The potential became crystal clear. Clothing was an obvious choice to focus my time.

I still sell items on Amazon and eBay that are not clothing related but used clothing accounts for the majority of my business.

In the following chapters I will share a basic overview on what I have learned about selling clothing online, specifically on eBay.

Why clothing?

There are several reasons that selling used clothing is an excellent way to earn extra income. One reason I focused on clothing is because it is everywhere. Every thrift shop has sections of clothing for men, women, children, and babies. Most yard sales are full of piles of clothes people have cleaned out of their closets. In your own house there are probably countless items that could be sold. There are jackets that might not get worn anymore, business suits that might be in good shape but might never see the light of day. The trip to Hawaii when you bought a pricey Hawaiian shirt that sits at the back of the closet. There is someone that wants to buy that shirt.

Clothing is a necessity. It is not always the hottest seller or the latest trend. But everywhere around the world someone needs or wants clothing. Seasons change and people are looking to add a jacket for the winter or a bathing suit in the summer. In the spring, a golf polo might be a welcome addition to their wardrobe. The great thing about selling clothing online is that any time of the day or night, and every day of the week, people can buy from you. It may be someone looking to buy a non-iron Brooks Brothers business shirt in California when I am asleep on the east coast. People can shop anytime, day or night and never have to leave their house to do so.

Clothing is easy to store and easy to ship. A dedicated bookshelf can hold a couple hundred folded clothing items. This can fit in most people's houses. And to ship a piece of clothing, it is simply folded and put into a poly mailer envelope that costs a few cents and then is mailed USPS first class or priority mail. This is a very economical way to send things through the mail. Poly mailers are flat, cheap, and do not take up a lot of room. You don't have bulky inventory and boxes to ship.

Another reason to focus on selling clothing is that people are looking on eBay for a good deal. A designer shirt might be $100 in a retail store. Most eBay shoppers wouldn't pay $100 dollars for that shirt, but they might pay $24.00 for a nice used version of that shirt, and you purchased that shirt in the color and size they are looking for in a thrift shop for $2.00 - $3.00. It is a win-win scenario for both of you. You make a nice profit from the sale of that item and they get a great deal on the designer item with the cool logo that they have been coveting.

Perhaps the most important reason to focus on clothing is that it is extremely profitable. Typically used clothing items sell for about 400% - 600% markup. This kind of profit margin is what makes it so attractive. If you are choosing the right brands, you will consistently make this kind of profit, and you can even go over this range upwards of 1000%. Once in a while you might have some items that you need to lower the price to sell for 100% -200% mark-up but that is rare! Getting the correct items and brands is essential to a bigger profit margin. This all comes with practice. The more you buy and sell, the better feel you will get for your buyers' taste. If I spend $200 to buy used clothing I expect to sell it for $1000 or more.

Attached are some examples of items I sell:

Men's AMERICAN EAGLE Distressed Low Rise Boot Cut Jeans Size 38 x 32 — $23.00

Men's GUESS Cliff Boot Cut Distressed Jeans Size 42 x 34 — $31.00

Men's GUESS FALCON BOOT CUT Black Distressed Flap Pocket Jeans Size 34 x 30 — $27.00

Men's POLO RALPH LAUREN Preston Flat Front Khaki Pants Size 33 x 30 — $23.00

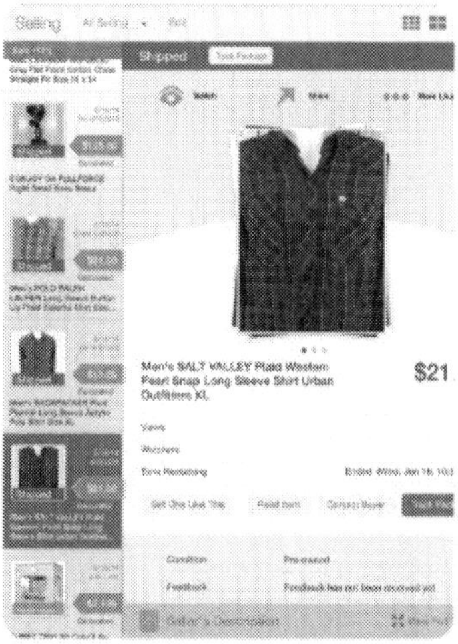
Selling
Shipped
Men's SALT VALLEY Plaid Western Pearl Snap Long Sleeve Shirt Urban Outfitters XL
$21

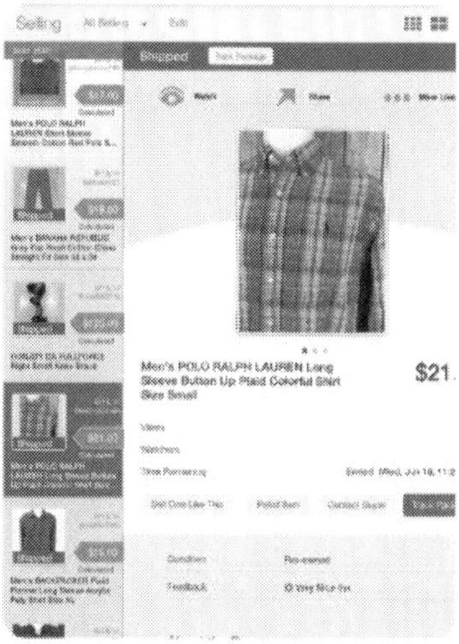
Selling
Shipped
Men's POLO RALPH LAUREN Long Sleeve Button Up Plaid Colorful Shirt Size Small
$21

Selling
Shipped
Men's AMERICAN EAGLE Vintage Fit Long Sleeve Plaid Pearl Snap Shirt Size XL
$20

Selling
Shipped
Men's NAT NAST Luxury Originals 100% Silk Short Sleeve Geometric Pattern Shirt M
$24

What do you need to get started?

Some of the items needed to get started you may already have, and some may need to be purchased. There are certain things that you may wish to add as you refine your skills. This section will go over the items that are the most important to have. Toward the end of the section I will go over the next phase items to add as you build up inventory and experience.

1. Digital camera / Phone - you will be taking pictures of the clothing items. I would highly recommend either an iPad or another tablet with camera. Typically I take the pictures of the clothing with an iPad and list the items on eBay using their app. It is much faster than taking pictures with a camera and transferring to a computer.

2. Shipping scale - A digital shipping scale can be purchased on eBay or Amazon for about $20. This is important to have before making any sales, as all items need to be weighed before postage can be purchased and the items shipped out.

3. Shipping supplies - Poly mailers are white plastic envelopes that close with a self-adhesive strip. These can be purchased on Amazon or eBay for only a few cents each. I use the 10" x 13" size for most shirts. Some heavier items such as jackets may require the 12" x 15" size. For pants I use the padded flat rate mailer from the USPS. They can be ordered on USPS.com and are free. Please note that you cannot get these at your local post office as they do not keep a supply on hand.

4. Computer and printer - You are able to list items via the eBay app on your phone and just recently they added the ability to print the postage to a wireless printer. However at some point you will probably find it easier to manage the shipping process with a computer. Most tasks can be completed via the app on tablet or phone, but some tasks can only be done via the full website.

5. eBay and PayPal account - An eBay account and PayPal account is needed to start selling used clothing. Hopefully you already have these accounts set up and have a general idea how eBay works. If not, it would be extremely helpful to read the portion of the eBay site called "selling on eBay".

Nice to have/ next level

These items are nice to have however they are not required in order to start out.

A. Mannequin or dress form - As with the other items a mannequin or dress form can be purchased on eBay or Amazon. A hanging mannequin is typically around $30. And a dress form is around $75. The dress form is free standing whereas the hanging mannequin is hollow in the back and requires something to hang on. The benefit to these items is that they add a degree of professionalism to your photos, as opposed to photographing the item on the floor or on a clothes hanger.

B. Light kit - A light kit consists of two lights with umbrellas that diffuse the lights. They illuminate the clothing items with a soft light and eliminate harsh shadows. In addition to the mannequin they add a higher degree of professionalism to your photos. The quality of your photos are very important because the buyer needs to see the best representation of what they are buying. This makes a big difference, can increase your sales, and also helps eliminate returns if they can see exactly what the items look like.

C. Steamer - A steamer takes the wrinkles out of the clothing and adds a professional look. Most items that you purchase from a thrift store get wrinkled from being tossed in a bag and not folded nicely. You can choose to wash everything you buy, or simply run the steamer over the wrinkled garments to freshen them up. If a buyer sees a wrinkled up garment in the picture they may assume that it is in bad shape. You can purchase a good steamer under $100.

How to find inventory

Building an inventory of quality used clothing items is essential. The more items you have listed, the more sales start to accumulate. Typically I sell around 2% of my inventory per day with a 'Buy it Now' listing. So if I have 100 items listed I can figure I will sell about 2 items per day. Weekends are better and can be twice that amount. The point is to build your inventory with quality used clothing and it is a numbers game. The more you list, the more you sell. It is as simple as that. The goal becomes building your inventory.

Starting out, search through your closet and find all the shirts, pants, jackets, skirts, or other pieces you could do without. They key is picking out mid to high end brands such as Gap, Polo by Ralph Lauren, American Eagle, and the equivalent brands. The better the brands, the higher your sales and profits will be. Perhaps teenager or children's clothing that would typically get thrown out or donated. These pieces are the start to selling used clothing online and a great way to build your inventory.

Thrift Stores

Thrift stores are the number one place to find inventory. There are chain thrift stores, private for-profit thrift stores, and small non-profit thrift stores associated with everything from churches to animal shelters. Each one of these types of stores has their benefit.

Chain thrift stores are nationwide or region wide at least. Goodwill and Salvation Army are examples of these. These types of stores are usually the biggest and have the most selection of clothing, and some of them have mass volumes of clothing. It takes time to go through the sheer quantities of clothing at these stores but your patience will be rewarded. Because they have so many donations, the odds are you will find some great pieces at these stores. The only downside to these types of stores is that they can be very busy and the prices are usually on the higher side. The potential profit may be lower at 300-400% markup. They are usually very consistent with their prices, leaving the potential to find some high end brands for the same as mid to lower brand prices. Ask your local stores about sale days. Sometimes these sales can be 50% off. You can really stretch your inventory dollar on those days.

Private for-profit thrift shops sound like they can be pricier but most of these types of thrift stores are looking to turn over inventory. Some of these thrift shops can be fantastic for finding inventory. They usually have sale days that are worth focusing on. The downside of the for-profit thrift stores is that they typically have a very good idea of what the higher end brands are and price them accordingly. So while there may be some hidden gems, they are the least likely to miss them. Still, there are several of the for-profit stores in my area and I hit them regularly.

Small non-profit thrift stores are the majority of stores. They benefit a church or charity. They usually don't have the volume of clothing items but they can be great for finding high-end items. Typically these stores price their items very reasonably and very consistently. They often don't differentiate a high-end brand button up shirt from a low-end brand shirt. They are one price for a type of item. Shirts can be $3.00 and jeans may be $4.00. No matter if they are True Religion jeans or Wrangler jeans and that can be a great opportunity. You won't find a ton of inventory to sell at these stores but the chance of finding some great items that sell for high profit are worth the stop.

Every thrift store that sells clothing has different methods for pricing and different levels of quality but they all have opportunity. Maybe they price their shirts high but their jeans low. Perhaps jackets or sport coats are lower in price. With some effort, you can find the reselling opportunity in every store.

Garage Sales

Garage sales can be a great source for finding inventory. Typically people having garage sales are looking to clear out space. I find that they usually throw clothing out almost as an afterthought. It is usually priced very reasonably since they are looking to just clear out extra stuff. I have found bins of jeans for $1 each or high-end business shirts for $1. Prices like that, you won't find anywhere else. The downside is that you may have to stop at several sales to get a decent volume. A good way to find garage sales is on Craigslist. People having garage sales will mention what they are selling in the ads. Also it helps to focus on good neighborhoods when looking for garage sales. The nicer the neighborhoods, the nicer the clothes are likely to be. I can't emphasize that enough.

Estate Sales

Estate sales can be useful because sometimes they can have entire closets of clothes for sale. They might have some very high-end jackets, dresses, shoes or sport coats, and since most people going to estate sales are focusing on antiques, there may be an opportunity for a great selection. You may even want to make a offer for the entire closet of clothes. The people running the sale might welcome that so they don't have to worry about getting rid of what clothing items are left over. You can find the good items and donate the rest for a tax deduction.

What to sell

What brands and what pieces of clothing should you sell? Well that is the million dollar question. Although I can't give you a list of items that are guaranteed to sell for maximum profit, I can point you in the right direction. Experience is the best education. The more you buy, list and resell, the more you refine your mental list of what to buy when you are sourcing.

Research is also the key to learning what brands and items to sell. There are two main resources that I used when learning what to buy to resell. Both the resources are free.

I recommend YouTube as a source for clothing reselling education. There are countless numbers of people posting videos of what clothing items they buy and the price at which they were resold. The key here is to double check what they are saying with the second method below. By using YouTube you will come across several brands or niches that you might never have thought about. For example you might watch a YouTube video by someone that resells men's sport coats or blazers. You may not have thought about reselling sport coats and don't know what brands to get if you did. Finding these people who have taken the time to make a video and post it online is worth the watching. They will give you a base of what brands to look for.

I also recommend eBay itself as a source for researching what brands and items sell well. Staying with the above example of sport coats and blazers, you can search eBay for what brands have sold and even the selling price of the jackets. The key is looking at completed sold listings. I also look at the listings that are currently for sale, but the completed sold list is what gives you the hard evidence on what has sold.

When you search for something on eBay there is a method to select only the listings that have sold. On the results page there is a box to check on the left after the listings show. On the app the selection is under the "refine" tab. Also, an easy way to tell if you are looking at the sold items is that the dollar amounts show in green. If you are looking at the items currently listed, the amounts will be in black.

Download the eBay app on your phone and take it with you as you hunt for clothes. You can quickly do your own research and see if the item you are looking at sells for a decent profit.

You will find most of this chapter will focus on men's clothes since that is what I sell. Although women's clothes are also a profitable niche, I don't have the experience to discuss which women's clothing to sell for the best profit.

The most basic item to develop an inventory and sell is the men's long sleeve shirt, either business or casual. They can easily be found at the sourcing places mentioned in the last chapter. After doing some research on brands on YouTube and eBay you might want to develop a mental list of brands. For example Polo Ralph Lauren, Brooks Brothers, Vineyard Vines, etc. As you flip through the rack, look for those brands as well as any with interesting patterns of material. These items are the most basic of men's staples of their wardrobe and a top brand shirt in great condition will sell for a great profit. Make sure the items are in very good condition or better. It is much harder to sell worn out items even if they are of a good brand. Sometimes the items may be stained, have a small tear, or be missing a button. At that point it is a judgment call on whether to spend the time treating the stain, sewing the tear, or adding a button. It should depend on the potential profit you can make from the shirt as to the amount of time and effort you put into it.

Other clothing items to focus on are short sleeve button up shirts, polo shirts, pants, and jeans. These are the basic items to build up your inventory. As with the long sleeve shirt, pick an item and start researching what sells in that category. It may be helpful to start a written (or maybe just mental) list of the brands that you are looking for. Even better, memorize the tag design so you can pick it out quickly while flipping through the racks.

Sometimes you will come across a tag name that you don't recognize from your research. When you first start this business you will come across them more frequently. This is where it is handy to have an android or Apple phone with the eBay app. Then you are able to quickly look up a brand and see at what price this item sells. However don't get bogged down with looking up every brand. Just reserve this for a nice quality item that looks/feels expensive. You will see or feel the difference when you come across them.

After you establish a base inventory you can branch out into different or smaller niches. A lot of this depends on the area you live in. If you live in an area with a lot of coats and jackets in the thrift stores, that might be a niche you add to your inventory. I live in an area that has an abundance of golf shirts and Hawaiian shirts. Therefore I have added these two niches to my inventory and have learned to identify an expensive Hawaiian or golf shirt from a cheap one. As you add niches you learn to take what your region has to offer and it adds to your profits.

Trial and error is the final method for learning what sells and what does not. Sometimes you may research an item and list the item thinking it will sell but it ends up sitting out there longer than you would like. Since you didn't pay much for the item, you can lower the price and learn from the experience. This will happen even as you become experienced and you will constantly be learning what sells and what doesn't.

Trends may change, seasons may change and this can affect your sales. It is a business in which you will constantly be learning and adding things to your "buy" list and taking them off as well. For example, when I started Tommy Bahama was a great brand to buy and resell. As fast as I could find them I would buy and resell these shirts. Then a couple things happened, first the thrift stores started to realize these shirts were very expensive and started raising the prices of this brand. Then the brand lost its trend or the market was flooded with these shirts and the resale price dropped significantly. So naturally I stopped buying that brand of shirt, but not before I had an abundance of them to resell and had to drop the prices. I didn't lose money by any means but I did not resell them for my target percentage either.

In this business it is extremely helpful to be aware of trends and classic styles of clothing. Be aware of what clothing people are wearing and it will help you identify what to buy and resell.

How to sell

I have gone over why to sell clothing and what clothing to look for, now we are going to look at how to actually list and sell the clothing items. These are the steps I follow but you can do what works for you. This is just a guideline that can make it easier to get started. I usually work through the steps with a group of items. Not just one item at a time. I typically work with about 20 items at a time. You may want to work with less or more depending on your preference.

1. Photograph the clothing items. Once the clothing pieces are brought home I wash any items that may need washing because they are dingy or have some small stains that need to be treated and washed. Shirts and jackets are photographed on the mannequin and pants and jeans are photographed on the floor. For shirts and jackets I photograph each item a few times. First a long shot to show the whole item, then a mid shot to show a closer look at the pattern, and finally a closer shot to show the tag. Below is an example of some photographs.

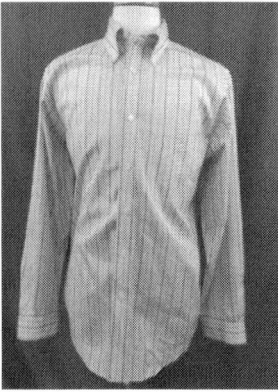

The process is a little different with pants and jeans. These are photographed on a clean floor, preferably a floor without a lot of pattern. I show the full front and back as well as the tag. Below is an example of the method I use.

2. Measure and document. The next step after photographing the item is to measure the piece and record the measurements. I typically take a few measurements for each piece and write them down along with a description of the piece in a notebook. For shirts, lay the item flat and measure the chest (armpit to armpit), the length (collar to hem) and the sleeve measurement (hem to cuff) for long sleeve shirts. For pants and jeans I measure the waist and inseam. The waist measurement is doubled since it is lying flat. Always measure pants to confirm the size that is on the tag. Probably half the time the measurements differ from the tag. Certain brands

are worse than others. These are the basic measurements that I take. Sometimes I will get a question from potential buyers asking for a measurement of the rise of pants or the shoulder-to-shoulder measurements. You can take these measurements on an as needed basis.

3. List the item. After photographing, measuring, and documenting the items you are ready to list them on eBay. In the next chapter I will give step-by-step instructions on listing with the app. If you need more detailed instructions for listing, navigate around eBay's listing process in the section called "Selling on eBay".

Some of the bigger picture questions for listing clothing are whether to use an auction feature or the buy it now feature which is a set price. I typically chose the buy it now feature unless it is an extremely rare item that you are not sure how much the item will command. Vintage items, sports jerseys, or super high-end items may fall into this category. Another question is whether to use free shipping or have the customer pay for it. I typically use free shipping and bump the price of the item up to cover the cost of shipping. Some people lower the price and have the customer pay for shipping. I have read that eBay gives preference to the free shipping in their search algorithm but I am not sure about that.

You should try different versions to see what might work best with your niche and target market. One note is to always fully describe your item and note any flaws in the item. It will help you out in the long run in making sure the customer knows exactly what to expect and it will cut back on the amount of returns you get.

Set goals on listing items. It can be one of the more laborious parts of the business but it is a numbers game. The more you list, the more you sell. It really is that simple. Set a goal for a certain number of items to list by the day or by the week. Meeting that goal makes you feel like you are on your way to building an inventory and selling items and it will also get you established more quickly.

4. Storage. You must have an organizational method to your clothing or it will be a nightmare to find things. Just folding the items and keeping them on shelves with like items can suffice. For example all short sleeve golf shirts together, all button up short sleeve shirts together, etc. Or if you have an extra amount of closet space you can hang the like items together. One method I use for pants and jeans is to fold the items and label the brand and size on a piece of blue masking tape and stick it on the folded item. (A word or warning, make sure you use blue masking tape and not regular masking tape, it can

leave adhesive residue on the pants. I learned that the hard way.)

5. Shipping. Congratulations, you made a sale! Now it is time to ship your item. The best way to make customers happy is to ship right away. Ship it the next day if possible. Nothing builds your customer feedback like speedy shipping times. Customers will be thrilled and let you know it by offering positive feedback and that builds your credibility and your business.

Use the poly mailers and print out your postage straight from eBay and get them in the mail. As you build the amount you sell, you can schedule to have the post office pick them up at your door. They will even provide you a tub for your daily packages. It really doesn't get much easier than that!

Under the 'My eBay' tab on your account you will see the number of items that need to be shipped. That means the customer has paid and the item is ready to go. If it doesn't show as ready to ship, don't send it out. That means the customer hasn't paid yet.

Printing the shipping is as easy as selection the 'ship this item' button. You then enter the weight of the package, select your shipping method and off it goes. On to the next sale.

6. Customer service and feedback. Feedback is what builds your credibility to others looking to purchase clothing on eBay. It says you are very reputable. The best way to build this reputation is by offering fast shipping, accurate listings, and excellent customer service. A lot of sellers make it very difficult to purchase from them because of their rules and policies. They seem to think they are doing you a favor in selling something to you. That isn't what you want to portray.

I suggest you offer the hassle free returns process. This will streamline any returns you might get, (and there will be some returns). As long as you are listing accurately there shouldn't be an excess of returns but sometimes the items just don't fit right. I make this suggestion: take all returns with a smile on your face. Don't fight the customers even if they try to blame you. It is not worth it. Take the return and give the refund and sell the item again. In the grand scheme of things, it is not worth the negative feedback to you to be "right". Some buyers might ask for a partial refund without returning the item. I typically turn these requests down and tell them they can return the item for a full refund. There are people who troll, looking for people to give them partial discounts for alleged flaws and stains. I just ask for the return and offer a full refund, but always with great customer service intentions in mind. We all have experienced poor customer service and it leaves a lasting impression. Offer great customer service and you will get repeat customers.

As you get more accustomed to photographing listing and shipping items, you will find a process that works for you. This process is not the only way to list clothing on eBay, but it has worked for me. You may find a completely different process of your own and that is ok, this can be a starting point. The point is to start and build up inventory and experience and in the process and you will develop your own procedures that work well for you. You will also develop a comfort level in the pricing of the items as well as different niches of clothing.

Step-by-step listing process

It can be daunting to start listing clothes on eBay. Where do you start? How does it all come together? Over the next chapter I will go over listing an item in the iPad app. It is also very similar to the phone app. It is easy once you get used to it. It just takes repetition to learn. It all starts by using the eBay app that can be downloaded for free.

The first step I take is to do a search for the item that you are ready to list. This does two things for you: it allows you to see what price similar items have sold, and it gives you a structure with which to list your item.

For this example I have chosen to list a pair of American Eagle jeans. I start by putting the brand and style of the jeans in the search bar. In this case: American Eagle Low Rise Boot Cut Jeans.

This will bring up the current listings so you want to select 'Refine' and select the sold items button. A screenshot of this follows.

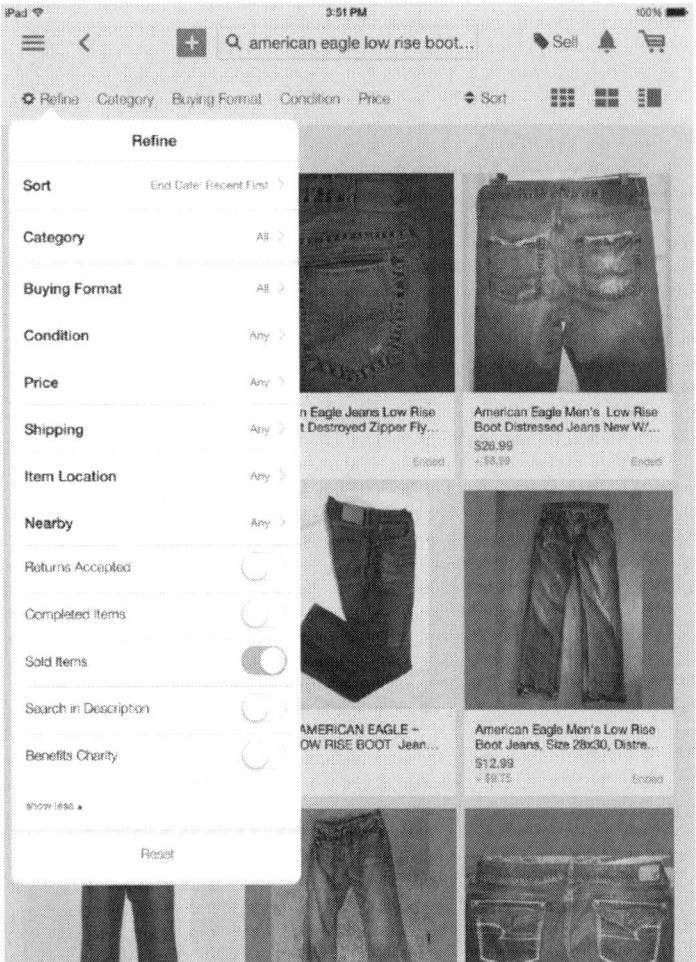

At this point you can see the price that similar jeans have sold for in the past. This will give you a good idea what price to list your item. One word of warning, the prices can be all over the board. Typically there are some oddball low prices that were probably sold at an auction. I never sell clothing at an auction because you don't make as much as a properly priced 'Buy it Now' listing. The only exceptions are very unique clothing items that don't have a clear history of sales. Everything else I list as 'Buy it Now'.

Next you want to select one of the listings. It will tell you that the item has sold and there will be a choice to 'Sell One Like This'. You want to click that button.

The following is an example of what this screen will look like.

This item has been sold. See more items like this below.

American Eagle Men's Low Rise Boot Distressed Jeans New W/O Tags 30/32

$26.99
Sold

See Original Listing

Seller's Other Items

Sell One Like This

Ended

More like this

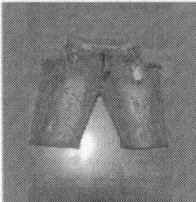

American Eagle Men's Low Rise Boot Distressed Wash...
$19.00

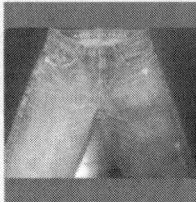

Mens AMERICAN EAGLE ~ Denim FACTORY DISTRES...
$16.99

AMERICAN EAGLE OUTFITTERS JEANS 32 W...
$16.50

American Eagle Low Rise Boot Distressed Jeans Men...
$9.99

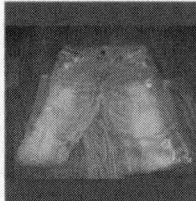

MENS AMERICAN EAGLE DISTRESSED DESTROYED...
$9.99

American Eagle Mens Size 29/30 Low Rise Boot Cut Sli...
$9.99

Structuring your listing

After selecting 'Sell One Like This' you will be ready to start listing your item!

The listing screen will consist of two columns, the left side showing the listing sections, and the right side showing the detail in the selected section. The first section is the title section. This is where you will enter a title for your listing, giving all the needed descriptions and keywords that someone may need to search your item. There is a limited number of characters that you can use for this title bar so make every word count. Basically, you want to put in words that someone might use in searching for that specific item. Include things like the brand, the style, the cut, the pattern, and the size.

Use as much information as you can, however don't just stuff it with words. The title has to make sense to the person reading it. I usually capitalize the most important feature, typically the brand. I don't use nonsense characters in the title to try and get attention. An example would be emojis, exclamation points or similar things. No one searches for those characters so they are a waste in my opinion.

I don't use the subtitle box as there is an additional listing fee and I haven't seen the benefit. The following is a screenshot of the Title section to use as an example.

Save & Close   Sell an Item   Preview and Publish

Title
Men's AMERICAN EAGLE Low Rise Boot
Distressed Jeans Size 36 x 34 ✓

Category
Clothing, Shoes & Accessories > Men's
Clothing > Jeans ✓

Condition
New without tags ✓

Item Specifics
Inseam: 32, Rise: Low, Material: Denim,
Wash: Distressed, Style: LowRise Boot,... ✓

Photos
3 photos ✓

Description

Format & Price
Fixed Price

Shipping

Title

Men's AMERICAN EAGLE Low Rise Boot Distre...

16 characters left

Subtitle

Optional - May incur additional fee

55 characters left

A title is a short description of the item you're
selling. Writing a good title is important
because **buyers find listings based on
titles.** Titles can be up to 80 characters long.
When creating a title, use multiple descriptive
keywords that clearly convey what you are
selling.

Subtitle

Capture the interest of buyers when they view
search results (in list view) by displaying
more information below your title.

I   The   Men's

Q W E R T Y U I O P ⌫

A S D F G H J K L Done

⇧ Z X C V B N M ! ? ⇧

.?123 😀 🎤 .?123 ⌨

Category

The next section to fill out in the listing is the 'Category' section. This allows you to categorize your listing in the correct area of eBay. For our example it would be Clothing, Shoes and Accessories>Men's Clothing>Jeans. This section also allows you to select a category of your store, if your have an eBay store. The following is an example of the Category screen.

Title
Men's AMERICAN EAGLE Low Rise Boot ✓
Distressed Jeans Size 36 x 34

Category
Clothing, Shoes & Accessories > Men's ✓
Clothing > Jeans

Condition ✓
New without tags

Item Specifics ✓
Inseam: 32, Rise: Low, Material: Denim,
Wash: Distressed, Style: LowRise Boot,...

Photos ✓
3 photos

Description

Format & Price
Fixed Price

Shipping

Preferences ✓
PayPal:
Returns accepted

Category

Clothing, Shoes & Accessories >
Men's Clothing > Jeans

Store Category

Men's Pants

–

Select the eBay category where your listing
will appear. When you select the most
appropriate category to list your item in, you
make it easier for buyers to find it.

Page 42

Condition

After the 'Category' selection, you will select the condition of the item. Usually the condition will be pre-owned but there may be times where you would select new with tags or new without tags. You may see the acronym NWT or NWOT in other listings. Those are common acronyms that refer to the condition of the item, New With Tags or New Without Tags. The following screenshot is an example of the condition section.

Title
Men's AMERICAN EAGLE Low Rise Boot ✓
Distressed Jeans Size 36 x 34

Category
Clothing, Shoes & Accessories > Men's ✓
Clothing > Jeans

Condition
Pre-owned ✓

Item Specifics
Inseam: 32, Rise: Low, Brand: American ✓
Eagle Outfitters, Wash: Distressed, Bott...

Photos
3 photos ✓

Description

Format & Price
Fixed Price

Shipping
2 shipping options ✓

Preferences
PayPal: ✓
Returns accepted

Condition

New with tags

New without tags

New with defects

Pre-owned   ✓

Additional item condition details

An item that has been used or worn previously. See the
seller's listing for full details and description of any
imperfections.

Some listing categories require you to
classify the condition of the item you are
selling. Please review the available options
and select the item condition which best
represents your item.

Page 44

Item Specifics

The next section is the 'Item Specifics'. The item specifics tab contains all the detail about the item that you are listing. It is a very important section because when people are searching for a certain item, the more matches to the item specifics, the more likely it is that your item will be displayed. This helps you in increased sales. If a size or color or pattern is left out, your item may not be found in the search. Although it is a bit of a mystery as to which items are displayed when someone enters a search, being as detailed as possible in the 'Item Specifics' tab surely can't hurt. In our example, the brand syle, and size are extremely important to list. The following is a screenshot of the 'Item Specifics' section.

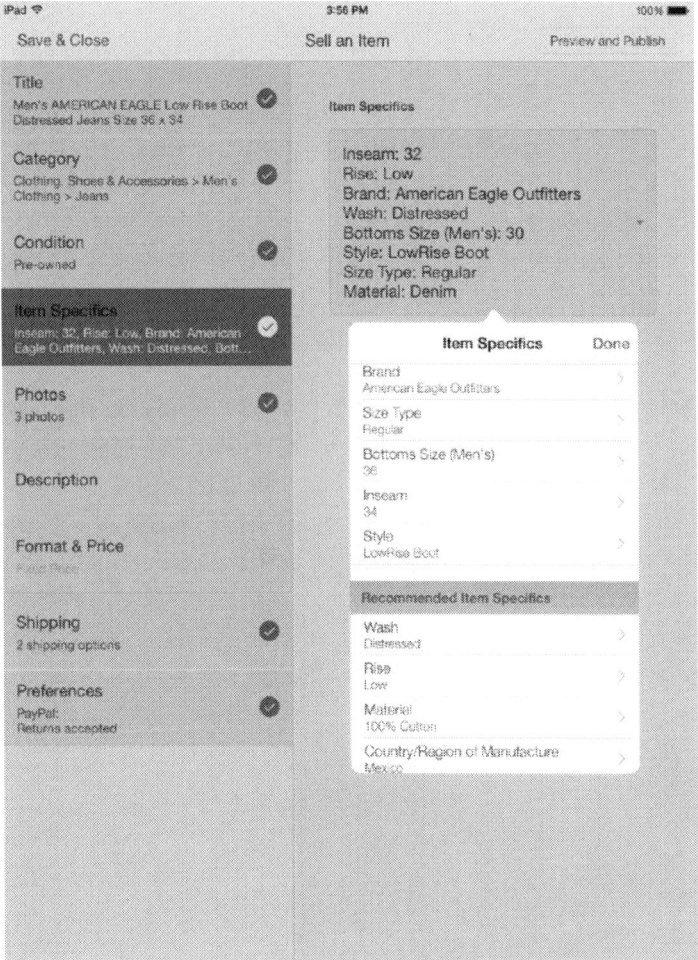

Photographs

The next section is the 'Photos' section. This is where you upload those great photos you took of the item. You can upload up to 12 for free, however I typically use only 3 to 4. Customers really want to see great pictures of the item so use as many pictures as you think necessary. This tab also lets you crop or rotate the pictures if you need to do that. If you have forgotten to take a certain photo, this tab even allows you to take a picture right in the app by clicking on the camera button. The following is a screenshot of the 'Photos' section.

Save & Close   **Sell an Item**   Preview and Publish

Title
Men's AMERICAN EAGLE Low Rise Boot ✓
Distressed Jeans Size 36 x 34

Category
Clothing, Shoes & Accessories > Men's ✓
Clothing > Jeans

Condition
Pre-owned ✓

Item Specifics
Inseam: 34, Rise: Low, Brand: American ✓
Eagle Outfitters, Wash: Distressed, Bott...

Photos
3 photos ✓

Description

Format & Price
Fixed Price

Shipping
2 shipping options ✓

Preferences
PayPal: ✓
Returns accepted

Photos   clear all ✕

Tap on the placeholder above to add new
images. Tap and drag to reorder.

Tips For Great Photos

Add up to 12 photos for free

On eBay, a picture really is worth a thousand
words — **buyers want to see what an item
looks like before they bid or buy.** Include
pictures of your item to greatly increase your
chances of success.

Tips

- To add a picture, tap on an empty
  space. You can take a picture using
  your iPad's camera (if equipped) or
  select a picture from your iPad's photo
  album.
- To remove a picture, tap on it and
  confirm.
- To reorder pictures, hold on the picture
  and drag.

Photo do's

Page 48

Item Description

The next tab is the 'Description' tab. This is where you enter your own words on the general description of the item. I usually use this area to summarize what the item is, what size it is, and the condition of the item. Also I put the measurements of the garment that I have taken. Common terms for the condition of the items are excellent used condition, very good used condition, and so on. Sometimes you may see acronyms like EUC to note the condition. I usually spell it out.

Remember to be honest with your assessment of the condition of the clothing. If you are not accurate it can come back to bite you in the form of negative feedback or increased returns. The following is a screenshot of the 'Description' section.

Save & Close   Sell an Item   Preview and Publish

Title
Men's AMERICAN EAGLE Low Rise Boot
Distressed Jeans Size 36 x 34

Category
Clothing, Shoes & Accessories > Men's
Clothing > Jeans

Condition
Pre-owned

Item Specifics
Inseam: 34, Rise: Low, Brand: American
Eagle Outfitters, Wash: Distressed, Bott...

Photos
3 photos

Description
Men's AMERICAN EAGLE low rise boot
cut distressed jeans. Size 36 x 34. Preo...

Format & Price
Fixed Price

Shipping
2 shipping options

Preferences
PayPal:
Returns accepted

Description

Standard	HTML

Men's AMERICAN EAGLE low rise boot cut
distressed jeans. Size 36 x 34. Preowned in
very good condition.

HINT: Tap the microphone icon on your keyboard to enter
text via voice. 🎤

An item's description provides buyers with
comprehensive details about your item. To
help buyers make an informed buying
decision, include accurate details of your
item's condition, any item defects and other
relevant information like brand names, model
numbers and dimensions.

Once the item is listed, you can revise the
item's description from the eBay web site to
add additional details.

Page 50

Format and price the item

The next section in the process is the 'Format & Price' tab. This section is where you will choose between an auction listing and a fixed price. I pick the fixed priced listing about 99% of the time. The price you are charging is entered in the 'Buy it Now' field. In the most recent update of the app, eBay will make a suggested listing price. I find that these suggestions are pretty accurate. They at least give you a starting point. Once in a while it will suggest an oddball price so just compare it to what you noted in your initial research.

One the duration of listing field, make sure that 30 days is selected and not 7 days. You want to give your listing enough time to get attention. I find that 30 days is the best. If the listing expires without selling after 30 days I lower the price just a bit and relist. The following is a screenshot of the 'Format & Price' section.

Save & Close   Sell an Item   Preview and Publish

Title ✅
Men's AMERICAN EAGLE Low Rise Boot
Distressed Jeans Size 36 x 34

Category ✅
Clothing, Shoes & Accessories > Men's
Clothing > Jeans

Condition ✅
Pre-owned

Item Specifics ✅
Inseam: 34, Rise: Low, Brand: American
Eagle Outfitters, Wash: Distressed, Bott...

Photos ✅
3 photos

Description ✅
Men's AMERICAN EAGLE low rise boot
cut distressed jeans. Size 36 x 34. Preo...

Format & Price ⏺
Fixed Price

Shipping ✅
2 shipping options

Preferences ✅
PayPal;
Returns accepted

Listing Format & Pricing

| Auction | Fixed Price |

Buyers are more likely to
purchase this item when
you list it as an auction.

Buy It Now $ None

To attract more buyers, list this item at or
below $18.00. Similar items that sold were
listed between $14.99 and $22.50.

Best Offer ⚪

More Fixed Price Options ▾

Quantity   1

Duration   30 days ▾

Schedule   Start immediately ▾

Enter a price in one or more of the price
fields. You can create the following auction
formats:

- **Auction**: In the Auction tab, enter a
  price in only the "Auction start price"
  field
- **Auction+Buy It Now**: In the Auction
  tab, enter a price in both the "Auction
  start price" and "Buy It Now" fields
- **Fixed Price**: In the Fixed Price tab,
  enter a price in the "Buy It Now" field

Page 52

Shipping information

The next section on the list is the 'Shipping' tab. The shipping tab allows you to enter the package information. The shipping type lets you select between a calculated cost depending on where the customer lives or a flat rate that can be charged. I select the calculated shipping.

The package details selection lets you enter the weight of the item as well as the measurements of the package. Here, the app usually selects the average for whatever item you are listing. For example, the app will select 11oz for a shirt. You don't have to be really accurate here. If you are charging for shipping, you want to be more accurate.

Under the Domestic tab you enter the shipping service. I always select First Class USPS for items 13oz and under, and Priority Mail for items over 13oz. This is where you would also select to offer free shipping. I offer free shipping and then adjust the price of the item accordingly. I find that free shipping is a great way to get more sales. I am not exactly sure why this happens but I am convinced it does. Some people list all their items with shipping as calculated. You can try the different choices and see what works best for you. The following is the screenshot for the 'Shipping' section.

Save & Close   Sell an Item   **Preview and Publish**

Title
Men's AMERICAN EAGLE Low Rise Boot
Distressed Jeans Size 36 x 34 ✓

Category
Clothing, Shoes & Accessories > Men's
Clothing > Jeans ✓

Condition
Pre-owned ✓

Item Specifics
Inseam: 34, Rise: Low, Brand: American
Eagle Outfitters, Wash: Distressed, Bott... ✓

Photos
3 photos ✓

Description
Men's AMERICAN EAGLE low rise boot
cut distressed jeans. Size 36 x 34. Preo... ✓

Format & Price
Fixed Price, $21.99 ✓

Shipping
2 shipping options ✓

Preferences
PayPal
Returns accepted ✓

Domestic Shipping

Shipment Type
Calculated: Cost varies by buyer location ⌄

Package Details
Package (or thick envelope)
2lb - 7.0in x 4.0in x 4.0in ⌄

Domestic
USPS Priority Mail (1 to 4 business days)
$5.25-$11.55 varies by location
You pay for shipping ⌄

Suggested shipping option for similar items in
this category.

Add Shipping Service ⌄

International Shipping

Ship Internationally
using the Global Shipping Program

Simply ship items to the domestic shipping
center. We'll manage the postage and
customs process and send the item to the
international buyer.

Add Shipping Service ⌄

Specifying shipping costs in your listing is
vital to your success — buyers want to know
the total cost of the item before bidding or
buying. You can add multiple shipping options
to give buyers a choice of services and costs.

Page 54

Payment Information

The final step to listing your item is the 'Preferences' tab. This section is where you make a few business decisions. Your PayPal email address is entered so when people pay, the money finds its way to your PayPal account. I always select the immediate payment button to make sure the customer pays for the item before it shows as sold. I really don't know why this is a choice because if it isn't selected the customer can buy the item and pay for it later. The problem with that is that the customer sometimes forgets to pay or changes their mind. In order to prevent that, select this button and it requires payment ahead of time.

Another decision is the handling time and the returns accepted policy. I suggest a return policy of 14 days. A no returns policy is a big red flag to customers and 30 days just seems to long to me. The handling time I select is 1 business day. If you don't think you can ship items every day then choose a longer handling time. This just lets the customer know when they can expect you to ship their item.

The following is a screenshot of the 'Preferences' section.

Title
Men's AMERICAN EAGLE Low Rise Boot
Distressed Jeans Size 36 x 34

Category
Clothing, Shoes & Accessories > Men's
Clothing > Jeans

Condition
Pre-owned

Item Specifics
Inseam: 34, Rise: Low, Brand: American
Eagle Outfitters, Wash: Distressed, Bott...

Photos
3 photos

Description
Men's AMERICAN EAGLE low rise boot
cut distressed jeans. Size 36 x 34. Preo...

Format & Price
Fixed Price, $21.99

Shipping
2 shipping options

Preferences
PayPal;
Returns accepted

Immediate Payment

Require immediate payment through PayPal when a
member uses Buy It Now.

Item Location   United States ▼

Largo, Florida

33771

Handling Time   1 business day ▼

Buyer Restrictions

Buyer Restrictions block buyers:
* with 2 unpaid item strikes in the last month
* who live in countries you don't ship to

Returns Accepted

Donate to your favorite charity

Donate 10-100% of your sale to your favorite
nonprofit and eBay will give you a credit on basic
selling fees for sold items.

Make a Donation

By choosing to donate I agree and accept the eBay
Giving Works Terms & Conditions.

**Email Address for Receiving
Payment**

Specify your PayPal account email address.

Handling time

Specify the handling time for processing an
order after a buyer has paid for one of your

Page 56

Refine your skill

After you have some experience with the basics of selling clothing there are several areas you can focus on to bring your business to the next level. In this chapter I will go over a few that will help you take the next step and make even more money selling used clothing online.

1. Sewing buttons and cleaning stains. That might not sound like a good time but learning to sew on missing buttons and remove small stains from an otherwise excellent piece of clothing will make you more money. You may pick up a piece with a missing button on the cuff or a small grease or food stain that you missed. Rather than throwing it away or donating it, you can try fixing it if it can be a profitable item. There are times when I will buy an item knowing it has a stain or missing button just because I know that with a few minutes of extra work I can get a very good profit. It amazes me how many people just get rid of an item because a button comes off. This is a quick fix and if you need help, YouTube has great tutorials.

    Stains are a little more difficult to master

because there are so many different types of stains and so many different types of stain remover. What I have found is that the majority of stains can be removed with a mixture of Dawn dish soap, baking soda and a little hydrogen peroxide sprayed on the mixture once it has been scrubbed in. Treating the stains with this mixture and washing the item will take care of the majority of food and grease based stains. However with stains such as ink and paint it may be best to stay away. In my experience those stains are extremely difficult to remove if they are able to be removed at all. In that case your time is worth more than the potential reward.

2. Lower your costs. As you build your inventory and sell more clothing you will want to look at lowering your overhead costs. One way to lower costs is to become a top rated seller status on eBay. Obtaining this ranking will save you 20% off you selling costs. Becoming a top rated seller is achieved by meeting eBay's criteria for returns, shipping times, and other customer service related markers. It is not very hard to obtain this rating if you provide great customer service and have accurate listings. It will also give you a tremendous discount on shipping rates, which really makes a difference.

Another way to lower costs is to buy supplies in bulk. The poly mailers, tape, paper and other shipping related items can be purchased for a much lower price if you buy in larger quantities.

3. Open an eBay store. There are a few benefits to opening an eBay store for your pre-owned clothing , one of which is cost savings, and it will also allow you to better organize and showcase your listings. Buyers can search through all of your inventory in one place if they like an item that you are selling. This can lead to multiple item sales. Opening an eBay store will give you a certain number of free listings every month. There are a couple different size subscription packages and they can really save you money on eBay listing fees depending on how much you list each month.

Conclusion

This is a glimpse into why clothing is my preferred item to sell online. The market is far from being saturated because there will always be room for good quality high end clothing that can be purchased at a fraction of the price of which it 6060 60would sell new. Because this business can be part time or full time and run right out of a home, selling clothing offers flexibility that can compliment a job or even become your main source of income. It definitely did for me.

Good luck to you if you decide to give it a go. Just remember to stick with it and learn all you can from others who are willing to share their knowledge as well as your own research and experience. I hope this book gets you started.

Feel free to email me with any question at mclarsen888@gmail.com. I would be happy to help.

Printed in Great Britain
by Amazon